The Book of Kn[o]tsense

By Jerry Tomlin

Congratulations on purchasing "The Book of Knotsense"
I'm sure it will bring much enjoyment and entertainment
But first you will have to know how the book works
As you can see the next page has a cartoon but **NO** caption
Your task is to figure out what the cartoon is about before
turning the page to reveal the answer. I'm sure when the
answers are revealed there will be burst of laughter and
to some groans of " Oh! That is a really bad pun"
Hope you enjoy the book and watch for my new books
"The Book of More Knotsense" "The Book of Historical
Knotsense" "The Book of Literary Knotsense" and
"The Book of Modern TechKnotlogy" Have fun!

Jerry Tomlin

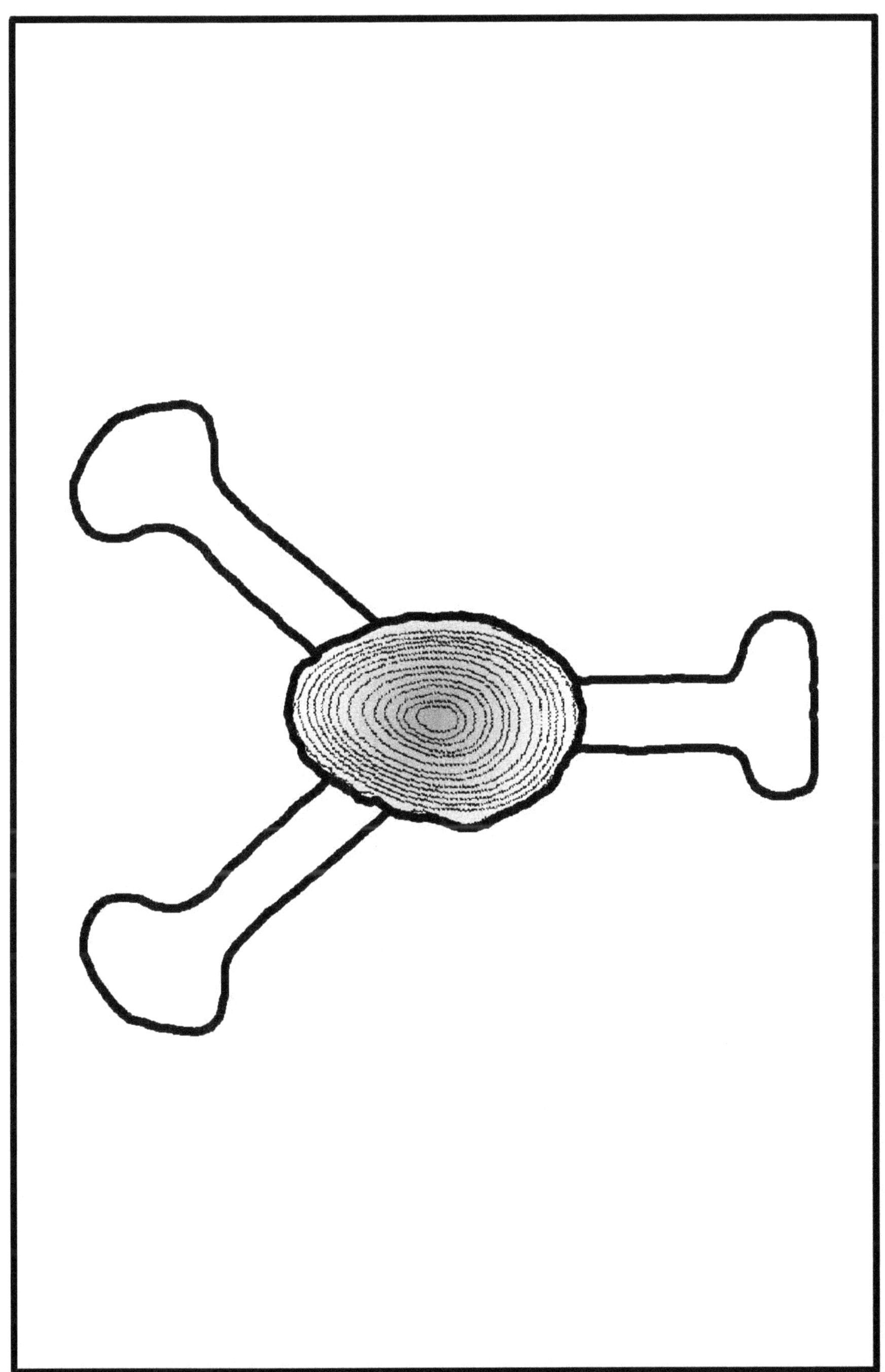

How did you do on your first guess?
Yes this is a

<u>Y-Knot</u>

And was the very first "What Knot"
as I've come to call them that I ever
created and started all this
Knotsense
So Y-Knot have some fun with them?

How did you do on your second
guess?
I know this one was a bit harder
But our thinker fellow is having a

<u>Knotvel Idea</u>

"What Knots"!

Who would have thunk it

Millions
YEARS

Knot in a Million Years

would I have thought that an original and clever idea like this would come to me out of the blue and hopefully bring me some Knotoriety

In God We Trust
Liberty
2008
In God We Trust
Liberty
2008
In God We Trust
Liberty
2008
In God We Trust
Liberty
2008

Besides there being a bunch of Knotsense in this book if you guessed right these are likewise

<u>Knot Cents</u>

I can see Lincoln turning over in his grave right now

It has been put in any number of ways
Knot playing with a full deck
Missing a few marbles
His elevator does Knot go all the way
to the ground floor
One beer short of six pack or

<u>Knot All Together</u>

I'M

KRAZY

In case some of you might think that
someone who dreams up weird or
creative stuff like this is a little strange
The one thing I can tell you is that
I'm not crazy, but definKnotly

I'm Knot Krazy

as in enthusiastic over "What Knots"!

BLAH!
BLAH! BLAH!
BLAH!

Our latest friend failed to keep all his Knots and bolts together and has succumbed to the pressure and stress of this crazy mixed up world and unfortuKnotly has become a

Raving LuKnotic

Where he has been tucked away in the.... ?

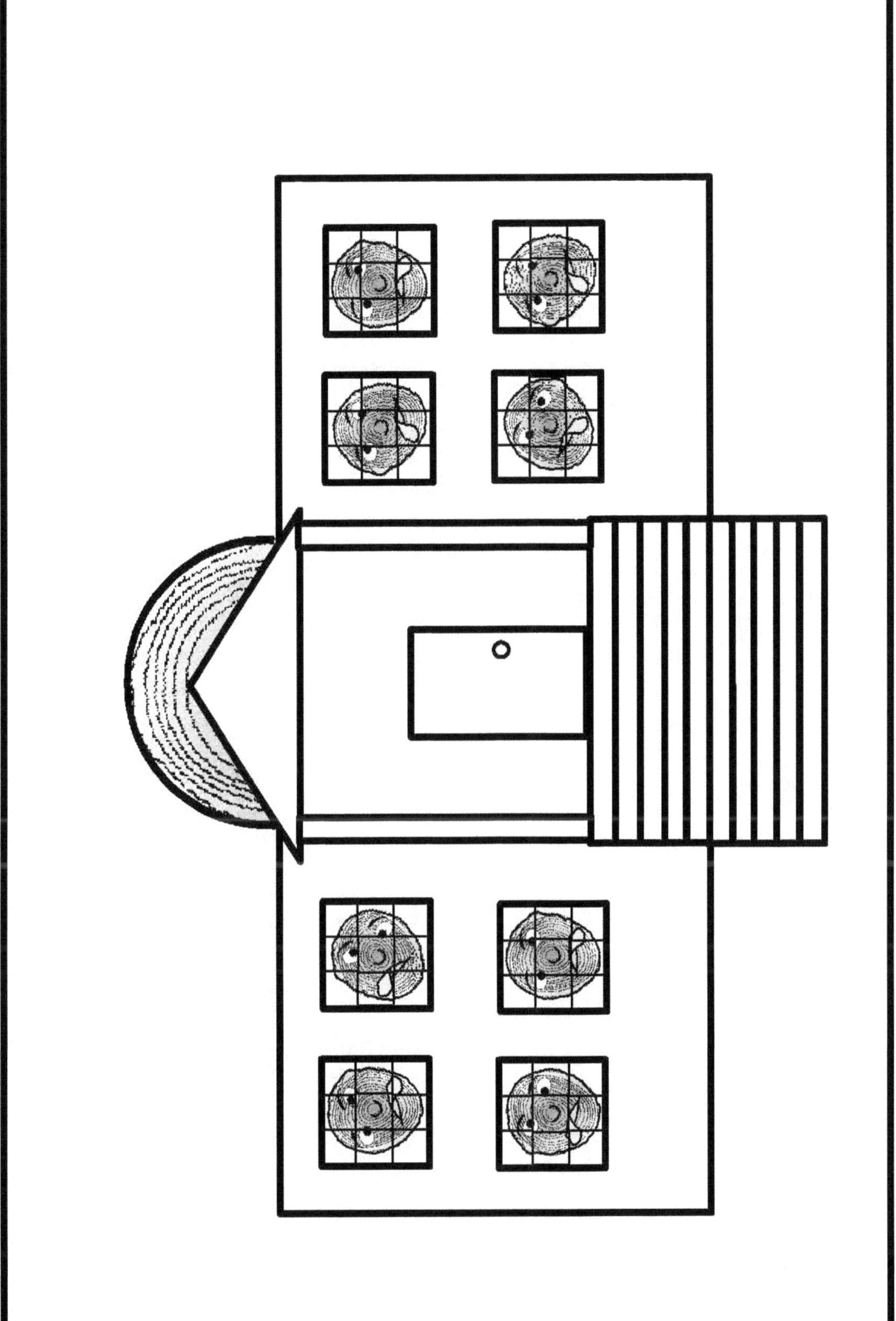

If you guessed what was the Knot so politically correct name it was referred to in the past as the

Knot House

You are correct although the more appropriate name is the

Insane Knotsylem

Good Bye
Cruel World
XXX

Some people get so depressed
that they may think about writing a

<u>**Suicide Knot**</u>

This book of Knotsense is intended
to be a tool to uplift and brighten
one's spirits when Knot feeling well

Note: The little x behind this person's mark indicates
that he be a Jr.

2
Worry

Should you be feeling a little down
in the dumps this "What Knot" says

Knot to Worry

Everything is going to be alright
Think Positive !

Soda
Pop

And to think positive the two words that should Knot be in your vocabulary are

"Can Not"

Yes! You guessed it!

This is a

<u>Can Knot</u>

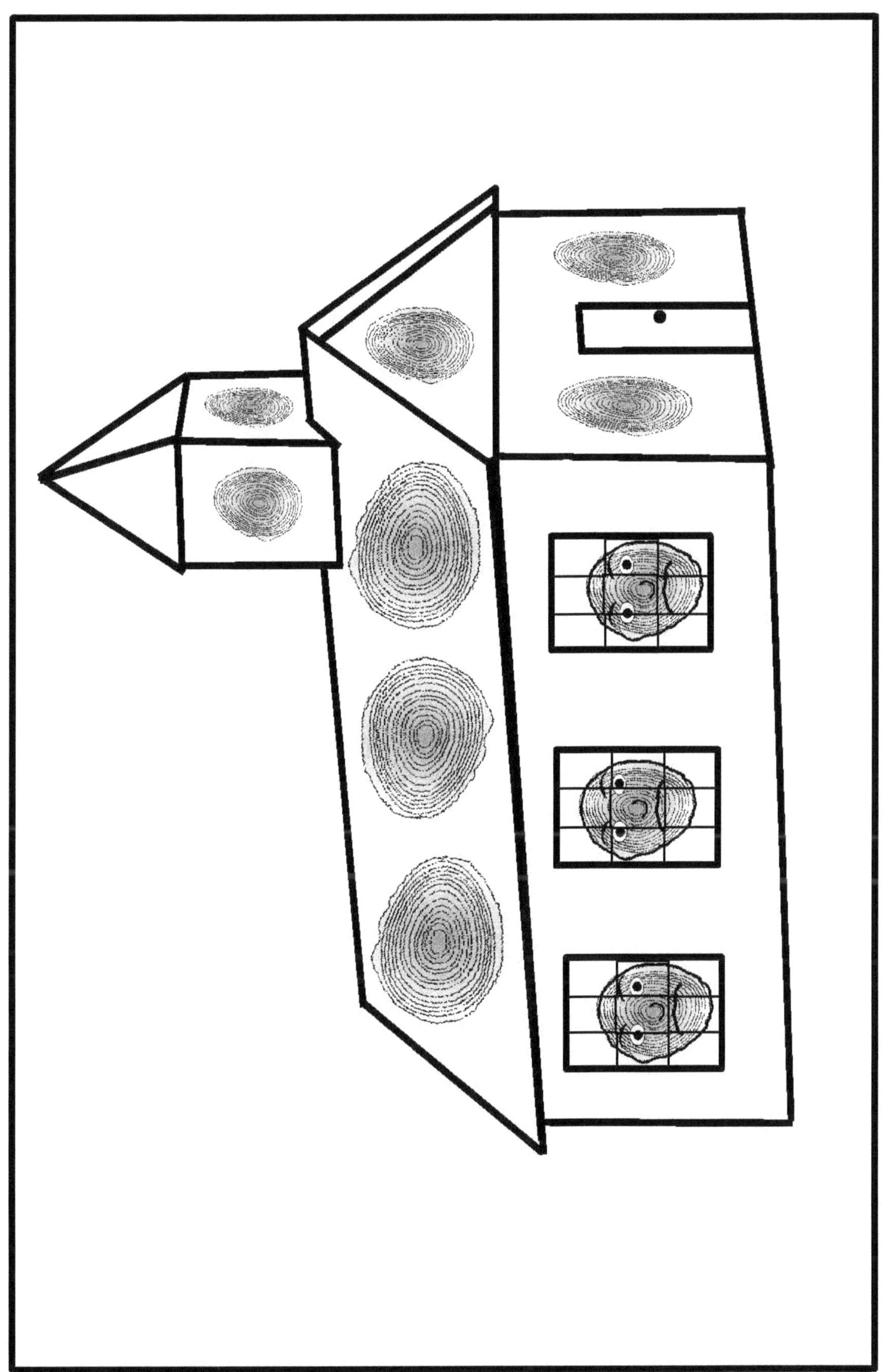

We have all had the experience
of going through the

<u>School of Hard Knots</u>

But should remember that life's
experiences are Knot always what
they seem and are placed there
for us to learn from and grow

Want

And with growth should come wealth and abundance so that you should be able to

Half Knot Want Knot

That's OK!

You can groan on that one

FEDERAL RESERVE NOTE
THE UNITED STATES OF AMERICA
THIS NOTE IS LEGAL TENDER
FOR ALL DEBTS, PUBLIC AND PRIVATE
F 35639229 L
WASHINGTON, D.C.
F 35639229 L
ONE DOLLAR

**George Washinton is
surely turning over in
his grave with this one
You got it a**

<u>Knot on Your</u>

<u>Bottom Dollar</u>

Who's There? Don't Chew...

I know you already got the
Knot Knot Who's There?

But!

Don't chew...think these
Knotsense Puns are
Hilarious?!

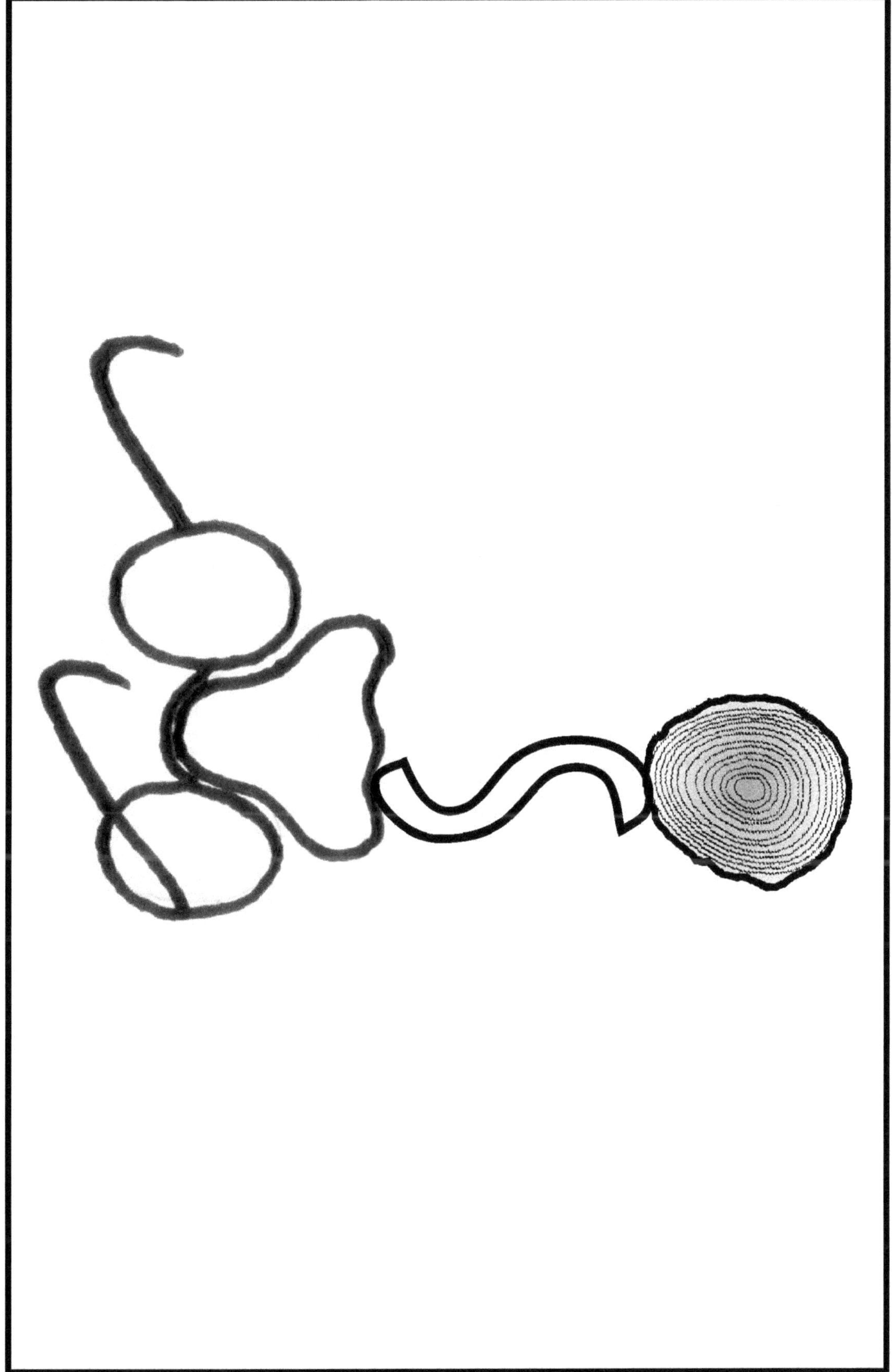

Had to slip in some bugger humor
When your lovin' with your honey
And your nose is kinda' runny
You might think it's kinda funny
But it's

<u>Sknot!</u>

Ooooew! That's gross!
I know, but it's still Punny

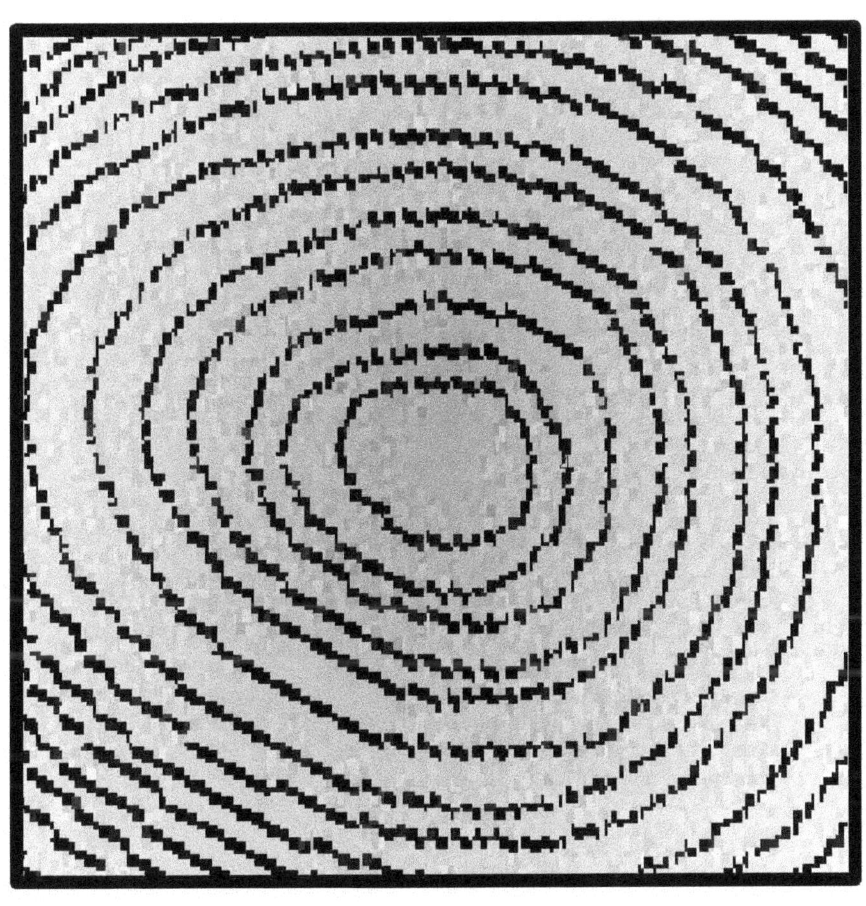

Any Boy Scout worth his stuff will
recognise this as a

<u>Square Knot</u> !

At four years I must hold the record
for being a Tenderfoot the longest
It's sknot that I lacked initiative but
was in it mainly just to have fun
And I did !

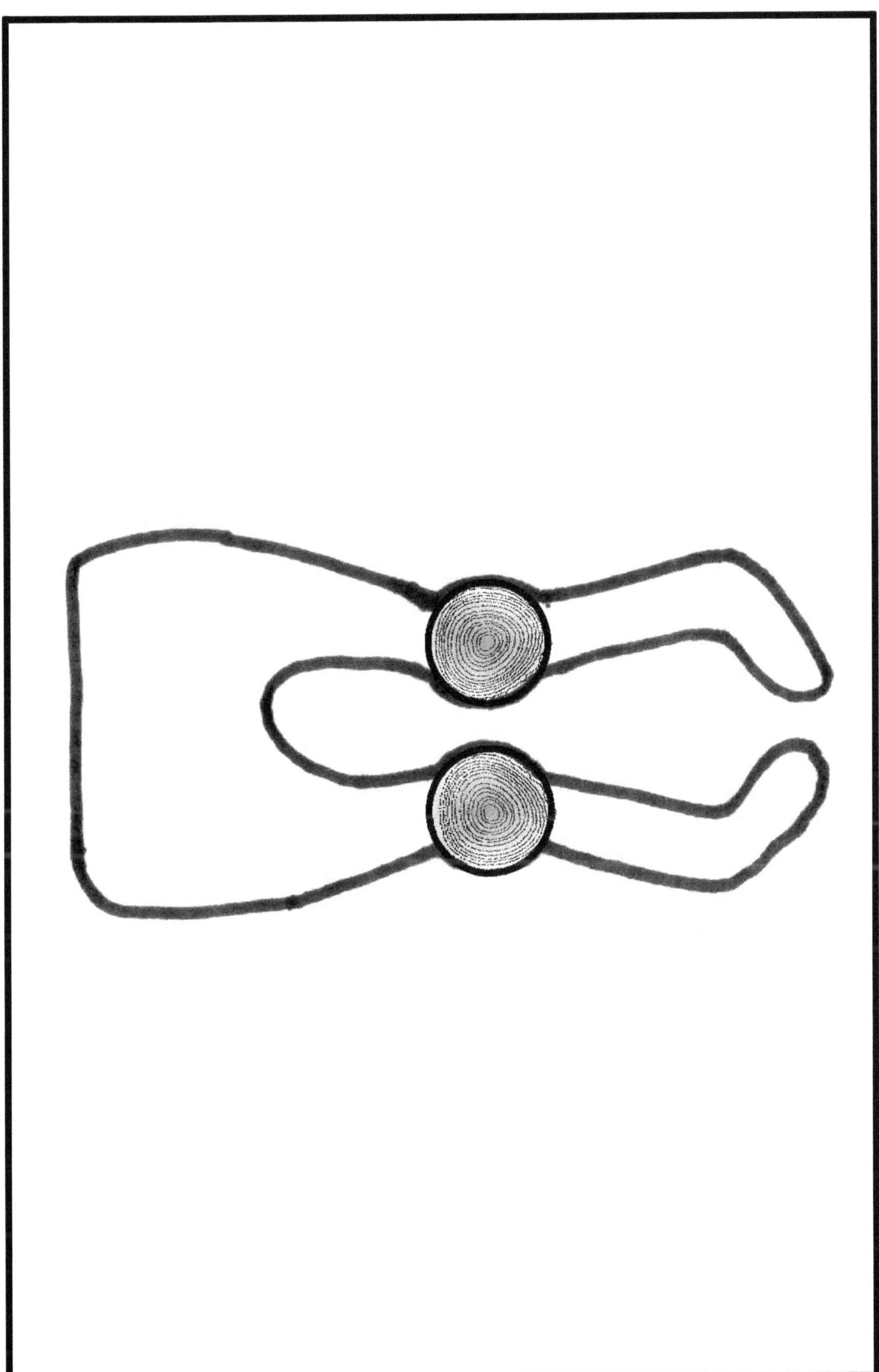

Wouldn't you say this
is the worst case you
have ever seen of
someone who is

Knot Kneed ?

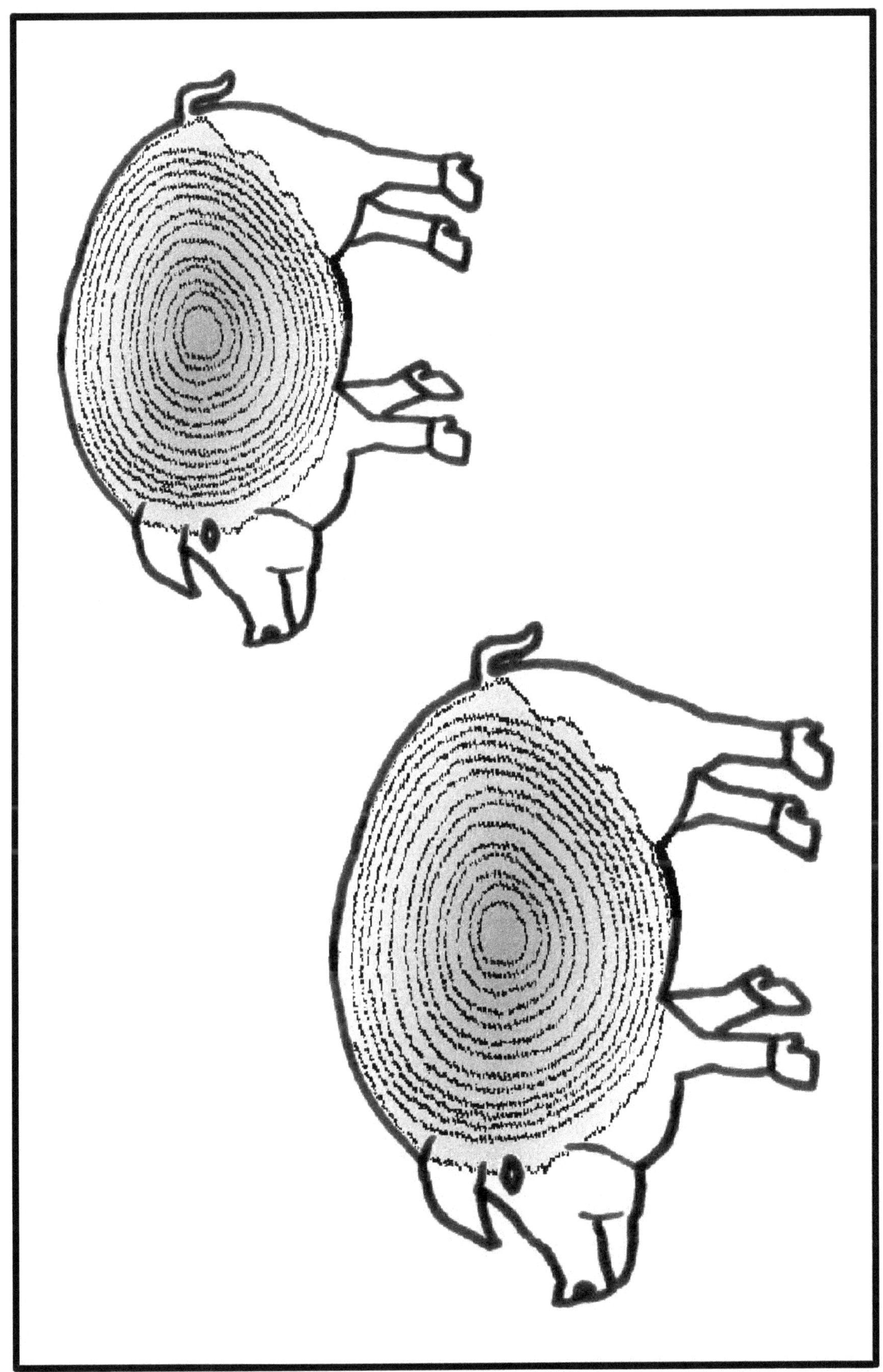

Once in my life I did eat what are
called Mountain Oysters
They were sliced like french
fried potatoes, breaded & fried
Actually quite tasty I might say
But Knot everyone knows they are
made from

<u>Pig Knots</u>

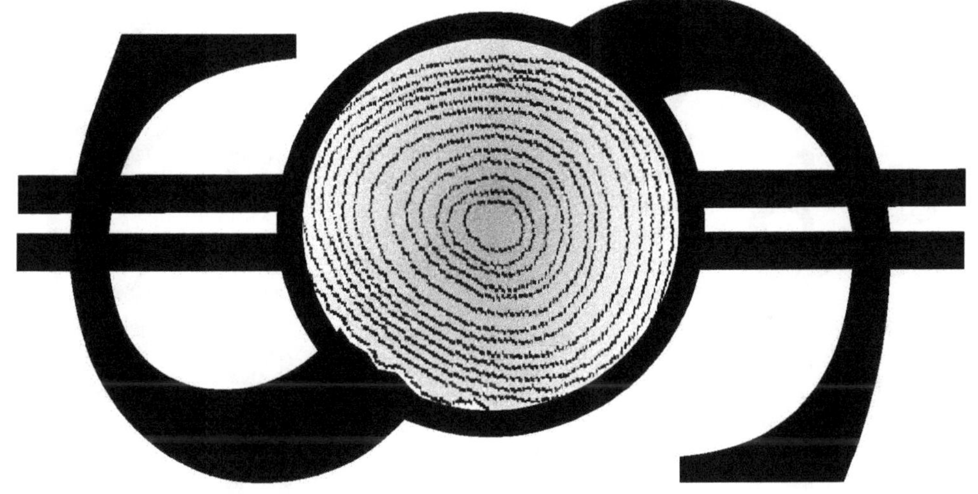

If you are a police officer
shame on you for missing this
one as it's a tribute to all the
jokes you endure about hanging
around the coffee shops
Yes! This one is a

Dough Knot

People should have principles by which they live and I have always maintained that I will only have a drink on days that end in Y-Knot Of course this "What Knot" is about the great support group

<u>Alcohics AKnotymous</u>

I'll drink to that !

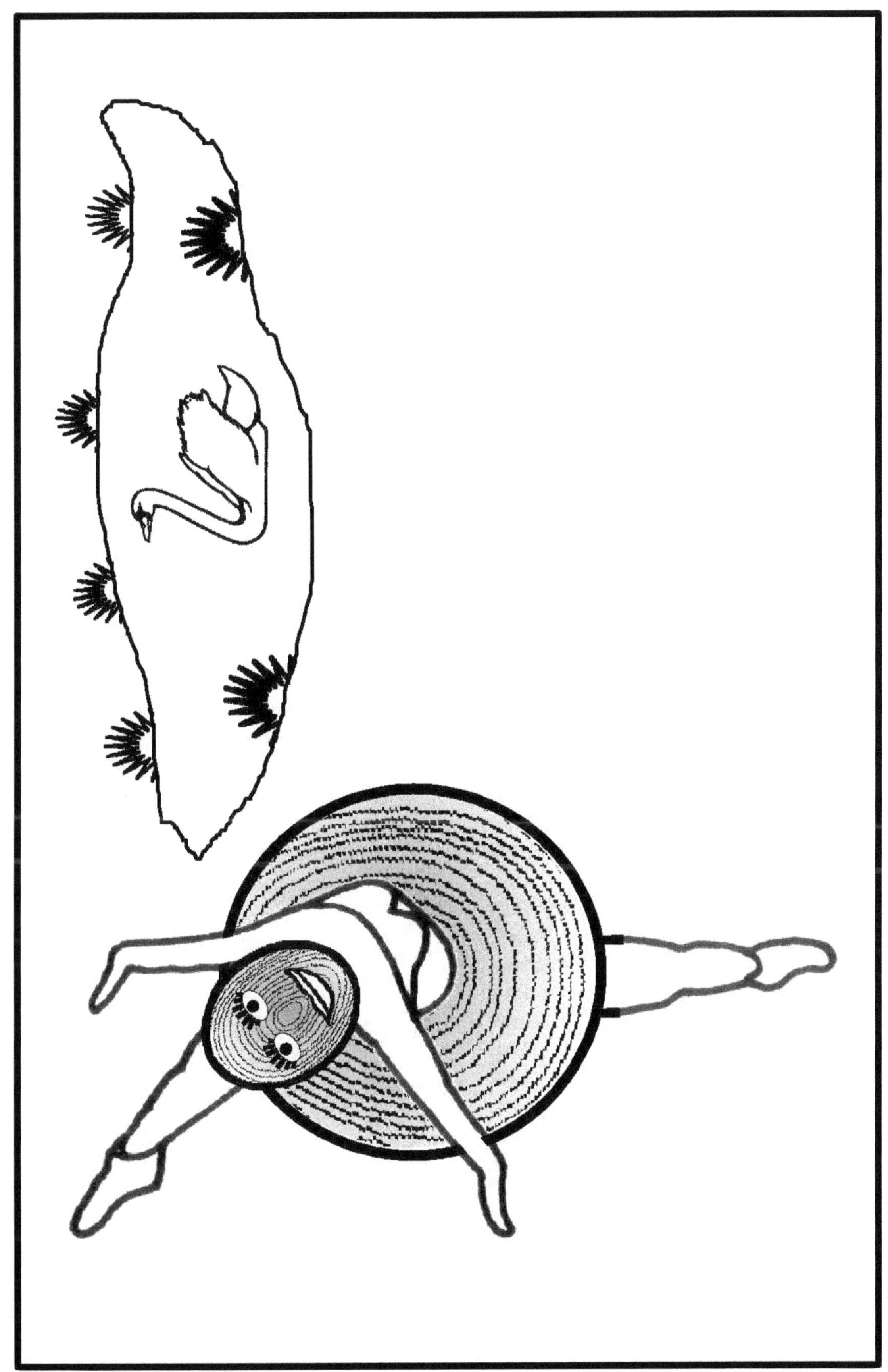

Anyone who has seen
the ballet Swan Lake
should have easily
recognised this
"What Knot" as being a

BalleriKnot

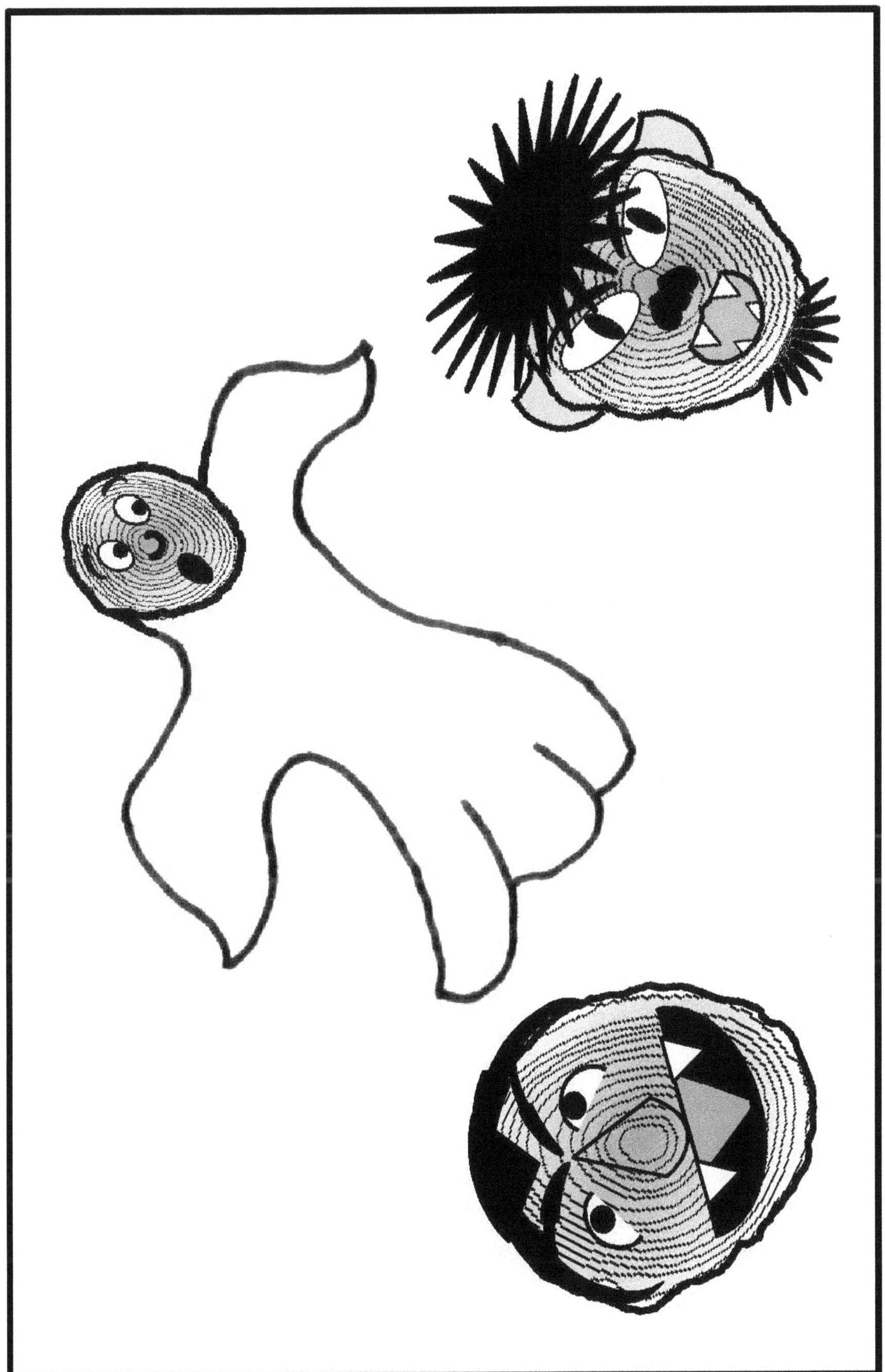

Vampires, Ghost, Werewolves, Poltergeist, Clairvoyance, ESP, and Mental Telepathy have always been associated with the realm of the

<u>SuperKnotural World</u>

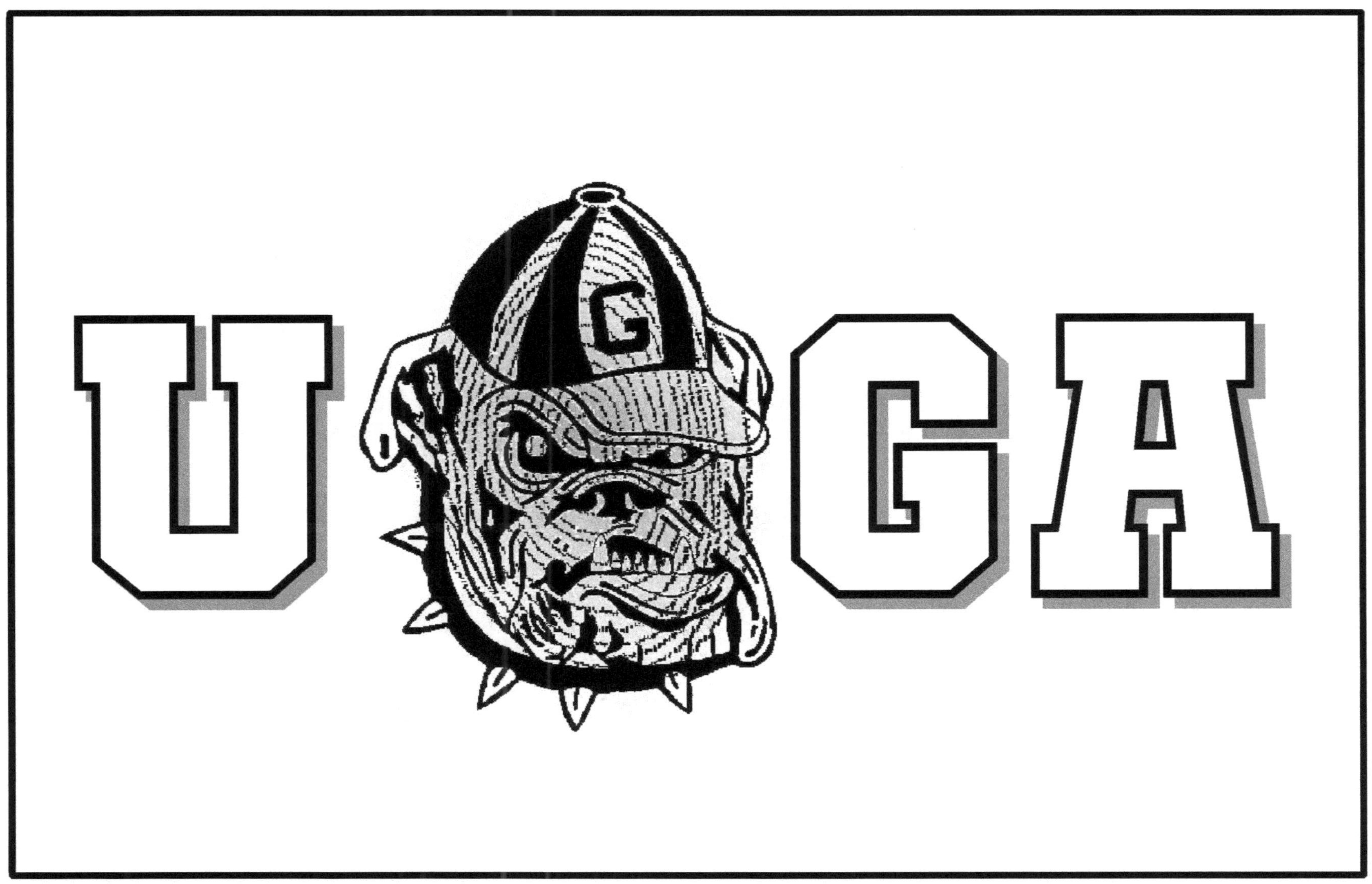
U GA
G

If you live in Athens, Georgia
or for that matter anywhere
else in Georgia as I do
You can Knot help but to be
a fan of the

UKnotversity of Georgia

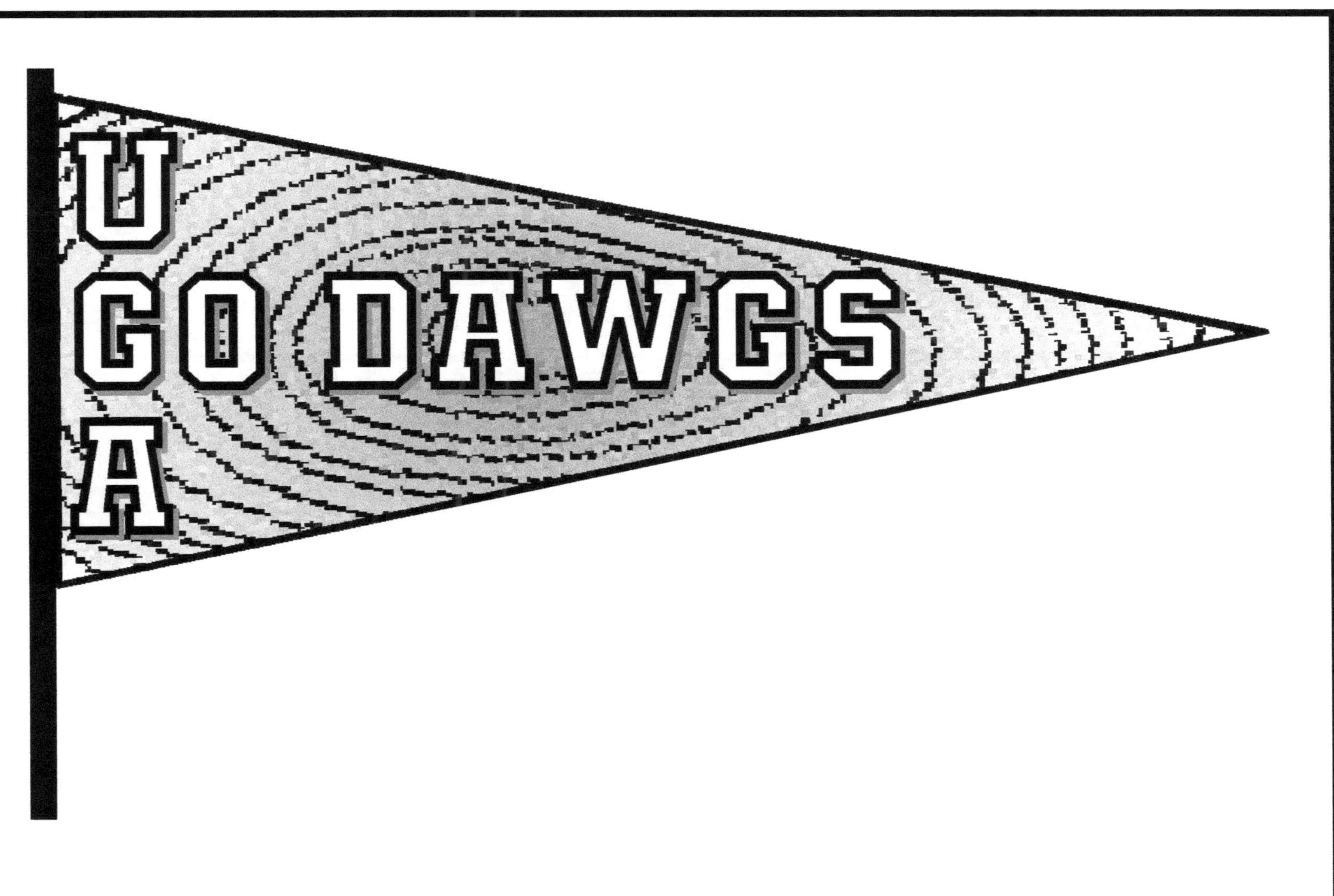
U
GO DAWGS
A

When you go to a football game
every fan that is worth his
salt should show his support
and enthusiasm by waving the

<u>UKnotversity PenKnot</u>

Go Dawgs !

OK! You have my permission
to groan on this one

Do I Know You ?
? I Don't Know

Once upon a time there were two people who had no idea the other one existed until by chance or fate their paths crossed and when they met you could say they were two lonely people who were

Strangers In The Knot

What Do You Think? Impressed?
Knot Only Brains But Muscles Too!

When two people initially meet one another for the first time there may be an immediate physical attraction
Hopefully the woman will be influenced and impressed with the

<u>MasculinKnoty</u>

of her new acquaintance

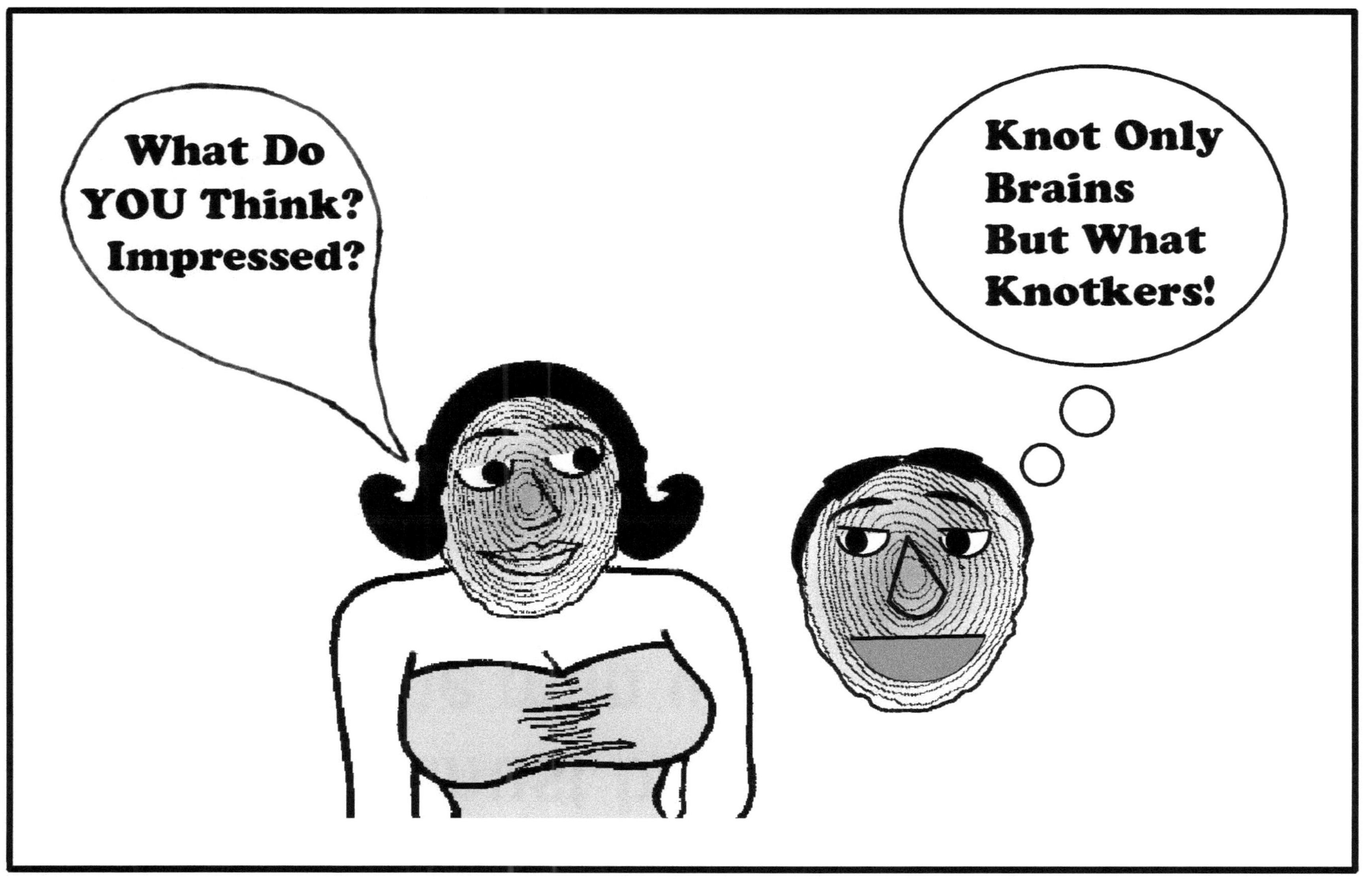
What Do YOU Think? Impressed?
Knot Only Brains But What Knotkers!

I know! It must be a guy thing but likewise the man will hopefully be similarly influenced and impressed by among other things the

<u>FemininKnoty</u>

and intelligence of the woman Young Dr Fronkensteen would have loved this cartoon

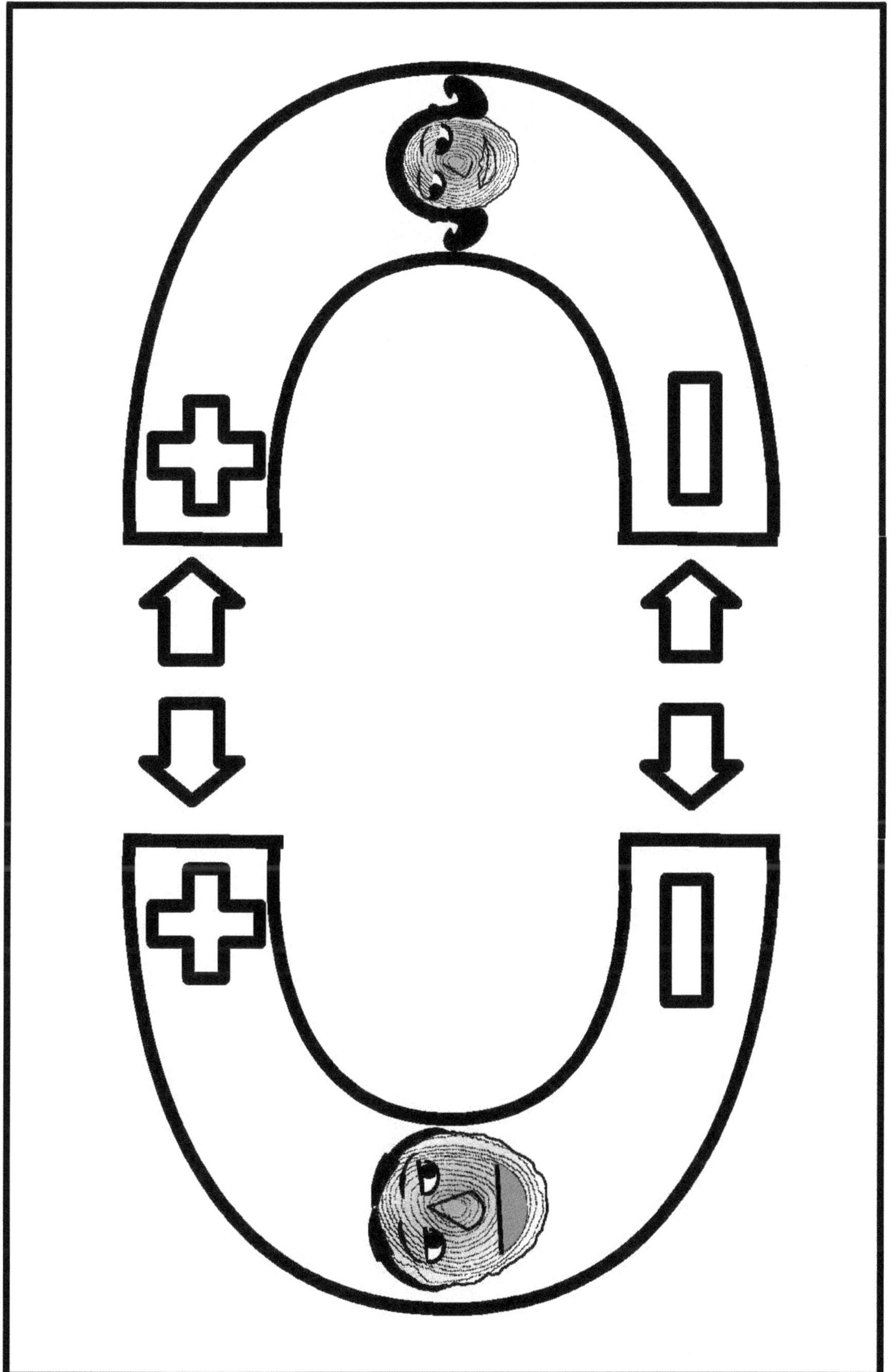

How true is the expression that
opposites attract?
Sometimes when two people meet for
the very first time they are attracted
to one another from the very start
But others may be pushed away as
are like poles of a

MagKnot

But polarity can be reversed

I Do Like You !
I Like You Too!

When two people do connect
and find that they have a lot
in common to share and
mutual values as well as things
they can learn from each other
then as the friendship grows
they might find they enjoy being

AffectionKnot

I
You !
Me Too!
N W?

When two people continue to build their relationship on a solid basis of friendship and trust then their emotions may become stronger and before you know it they may progress to being

<u>PassionKnot</u>

Ooooo! La! La!

As Lady Miss Kier would say

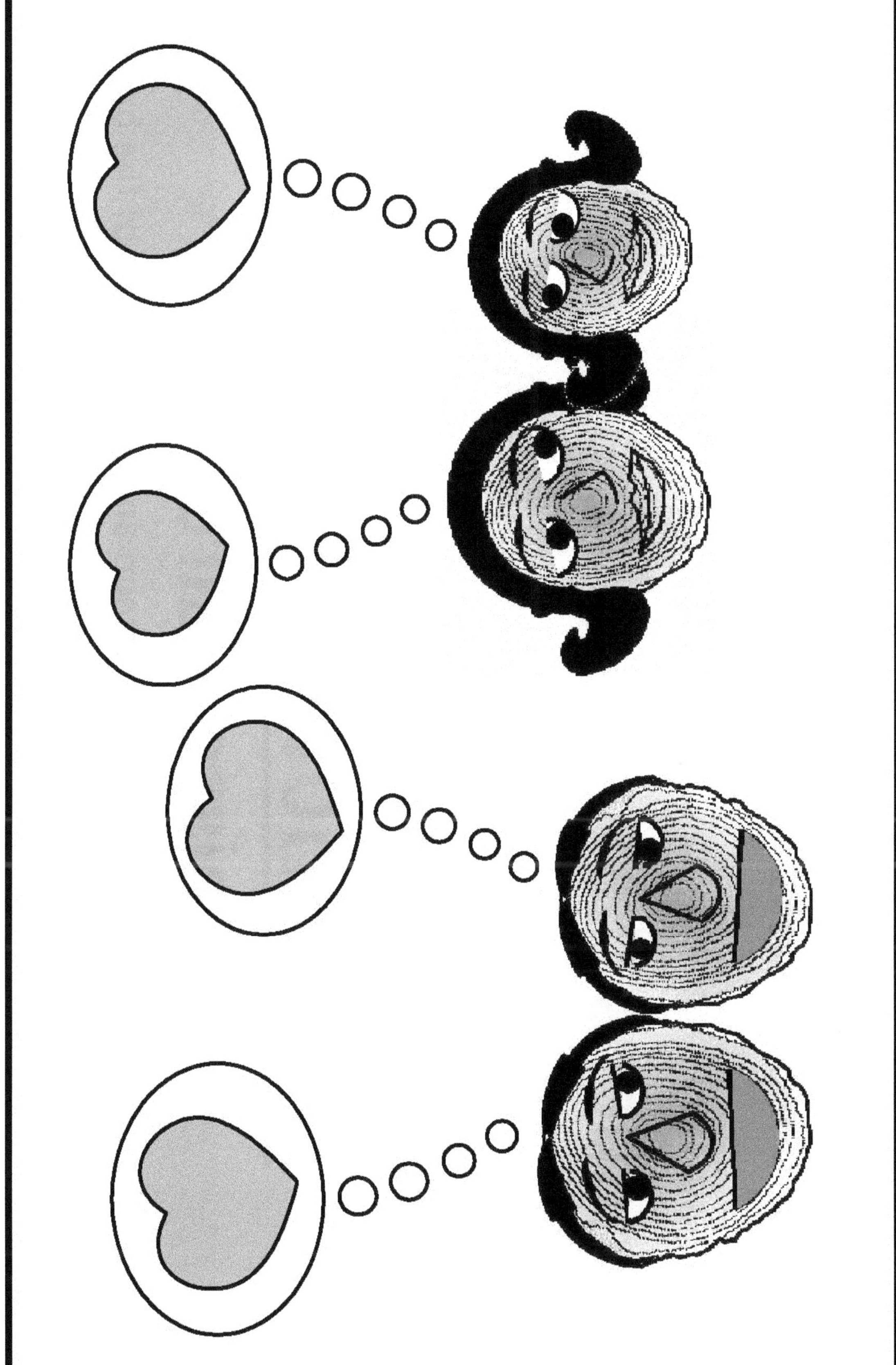

But everyone should recognise that passion and LOVE are uKnotversal emotions that all desire and need including those among us who choose to live an

AlterKnotive Lifestyle

Laissez-faire

Note: If you're offended by this one cartoon and like the rest of the book Just tear it out and get over it

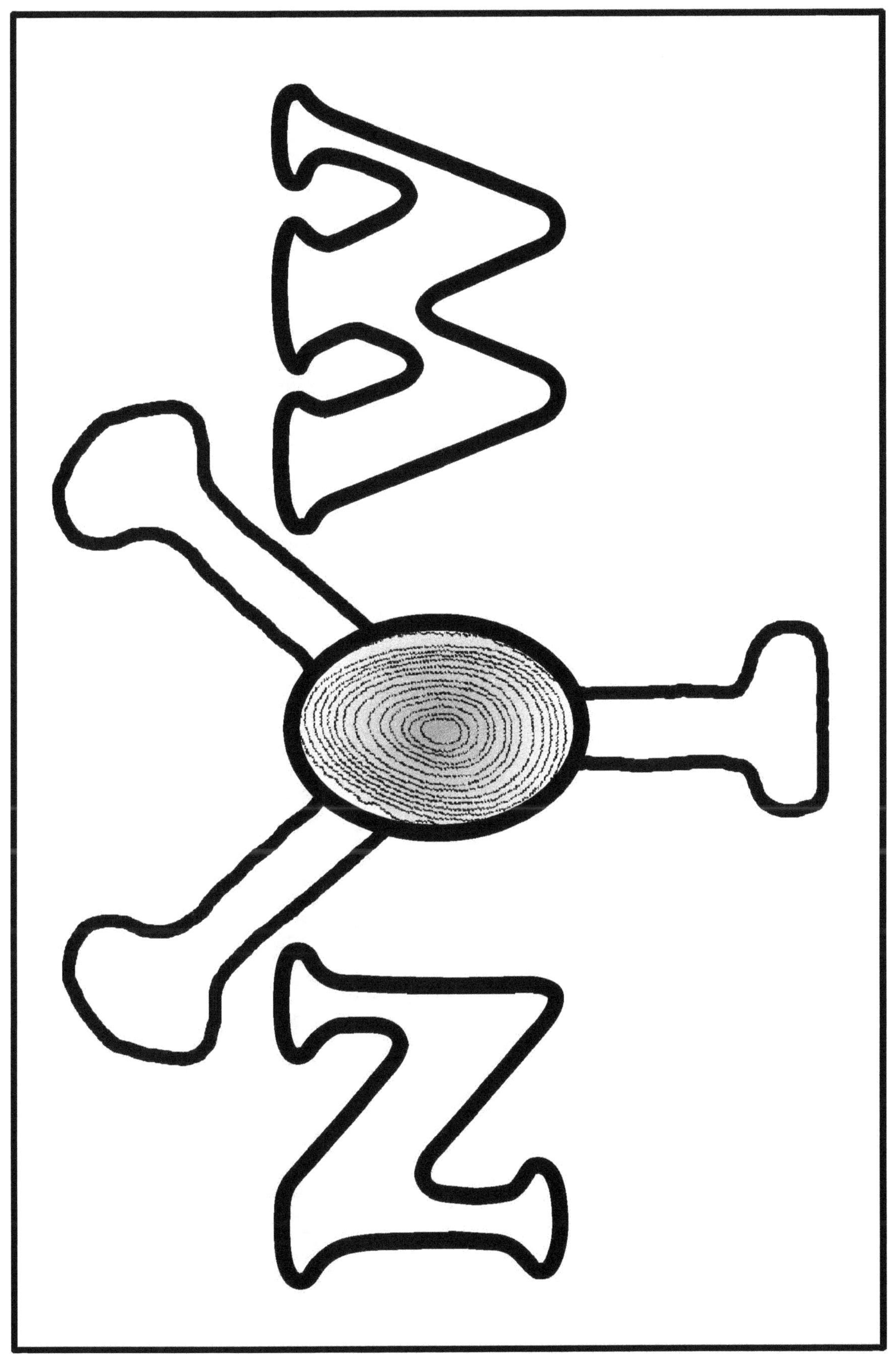

When all the positive and passioKnot
emotions are flowing one or the other
might often ask of their partner

THE Question

Y-Knot NOW ?!

And hopefully there will be a positive
response Whoopee!
As Bob Eubanks would always say

NOW

If you're getting the **Knot NOW** all
too often you might want to remember
that any fool can criticize, condemn
and complain and most fools do
Positive commuKnotcations that can
often times result in cooperation,
compromise and understanding will
always be your best alterKnotive

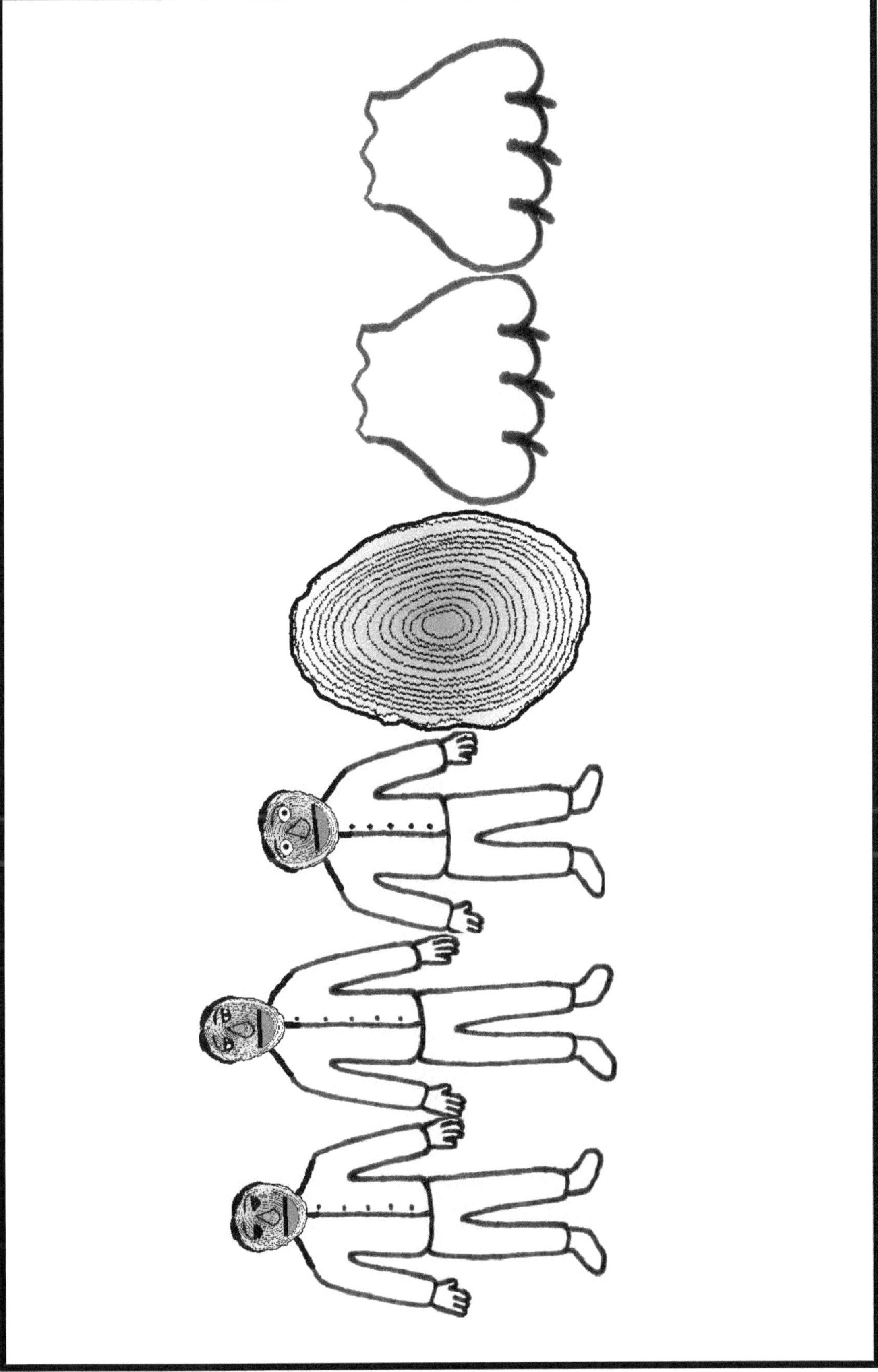

One reasons for getting Knot **NOW** is as a woman reaches the Autumn of her life she begins to have a different kind of hot flash which is associated with hormonal changes called

<u>MenKnotpause</u>

OK! I hear ya out there
But, it's been a while since a groaner

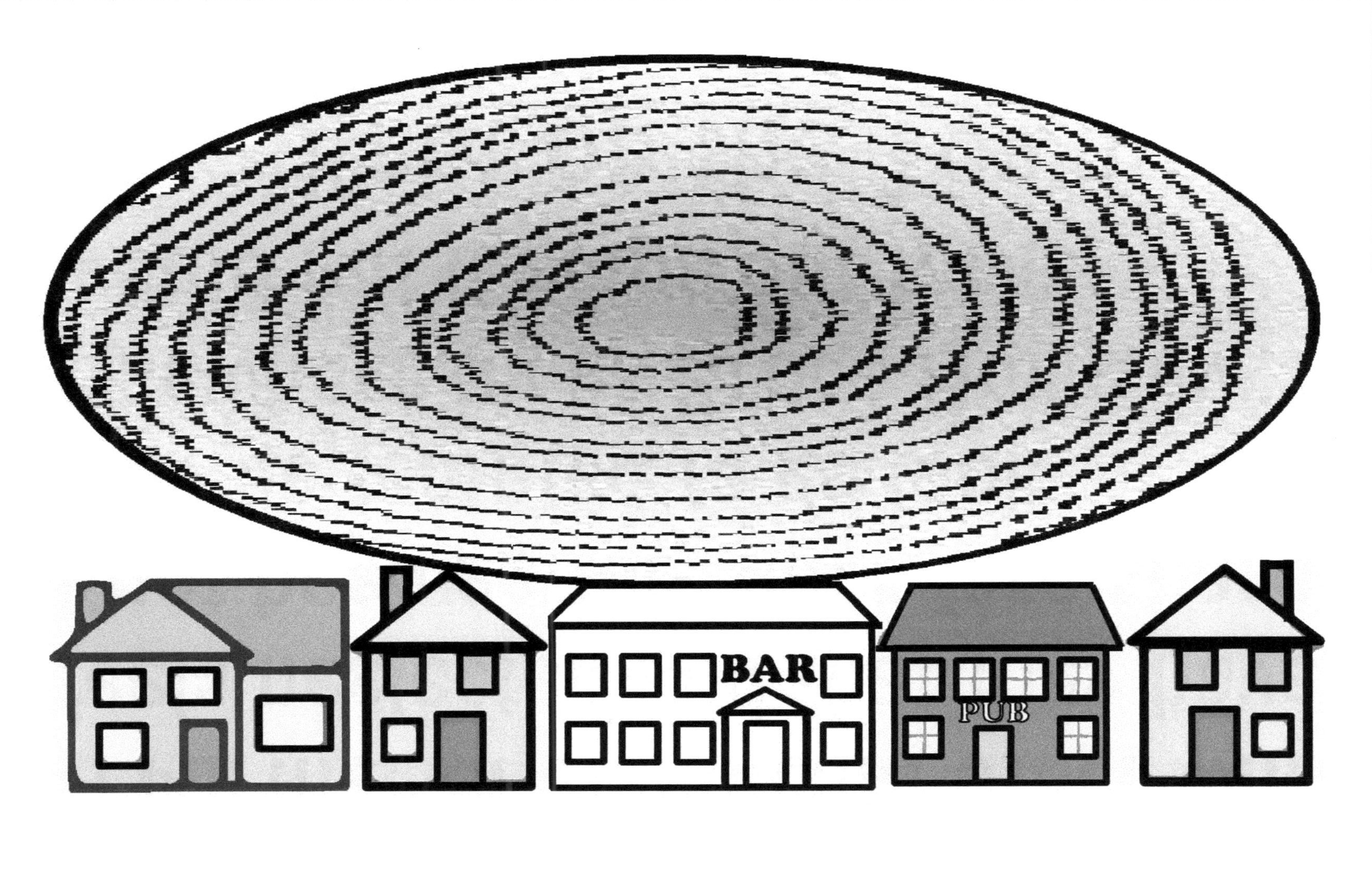
BAR
PUB

A partner or significant other who feels neglected and that they have Knot been getting their fare share may be tempted to go look elsewhere by as Bruce Hornsby would put it going out for a

<u>Knot on the Town</u>

And the bad thing about Knot NOW is that if one or the other partner hears it too often and goes in search of someone else to fulfill their physical and emotional needs then they may end up being

Knot T Knot T

And this is Knot a good thing for anyone to do

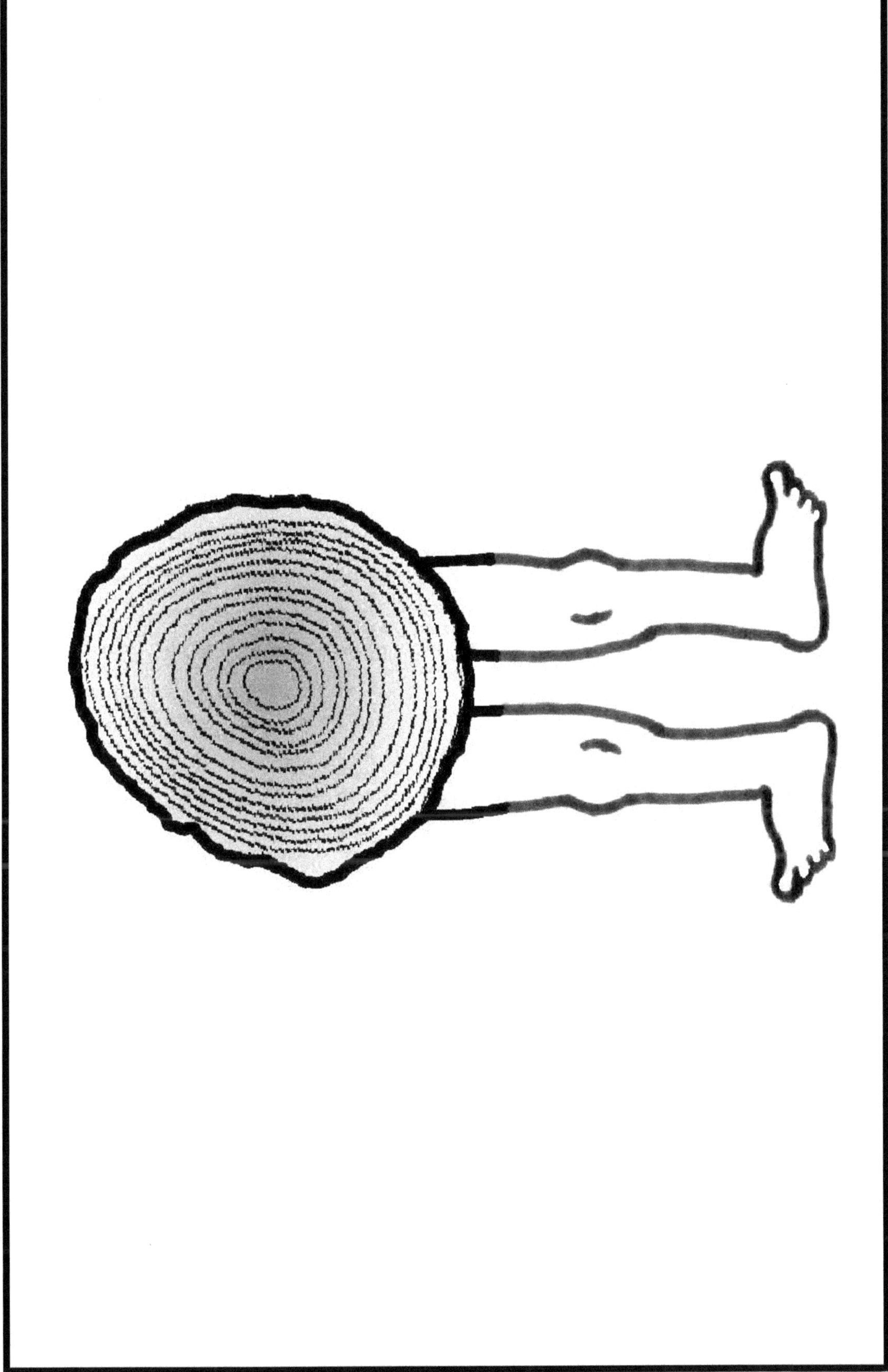

The unfortuKnot thing about being
Knot T Knot T is that many of these
affairs end up being a

<u>One Knot Stand</u>

Which usually does Knot leave either
party emotionally satisfied
And if too early in a singles relationship
as John Gray teaches in his Mars and
Venus books will usually end with . . .

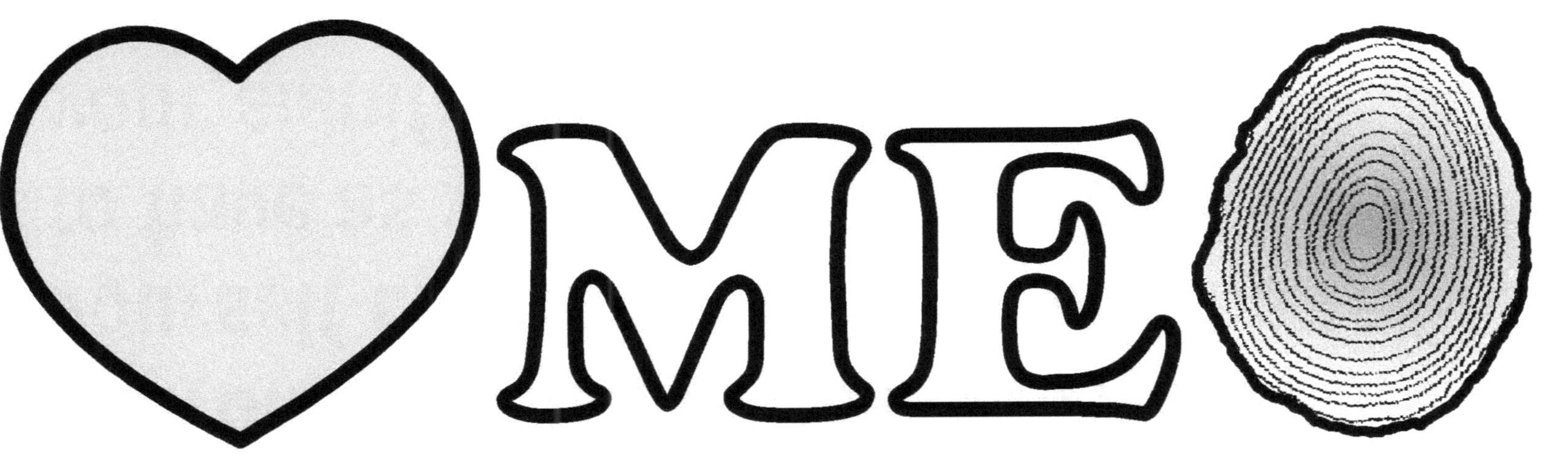
ME

. . . <u>LOVE ME KNOT</u>

When you bypass the steps of building
a strong friendship then you're setting
yourself up for failure and who better
to have as your best friend than
your significant other
So a word of sageful advice
Do Knot fall for the Knot T Knot T trap

You're The Only One For Me!
Me Too! N W ?

When both partners are committed
to one another and make a conscious
choice to be true to their one and
only significant other
Their relationship is called

<u>MoKnotgamy</u>

Do any of you remember the ending
to George Michael's music video?

We Never TRy ANything New!
Hey! M in knot Man KNot Now!

When both partners or in some cases one or the other lacks interest in keeping the relationship fresh by being creative and trying new things then their relationship is called

MoKnotony

Why Knot add a little spice back into your life toKnot! ?

DO
Disturb

Newlyweds know how to use this one

Do Knot Disturb

Of course it would possibly be useful
on a much needed vacation or second
honeymoon say to someplace like
Las Vegas to try and help break up
the MoKnotony

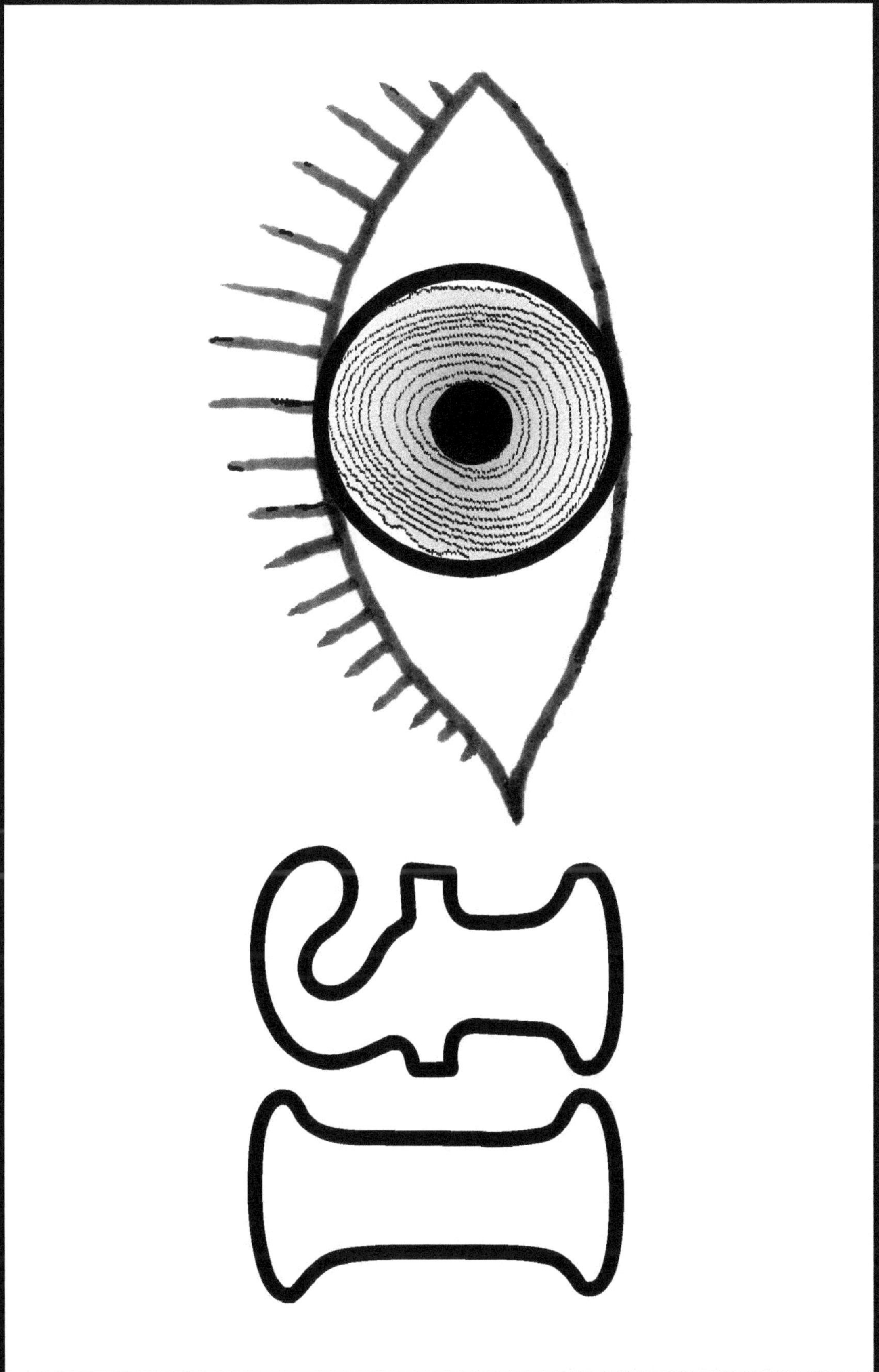

Perhaps you may have someone you would like to ask the question

If Knot I ?

Then why ?

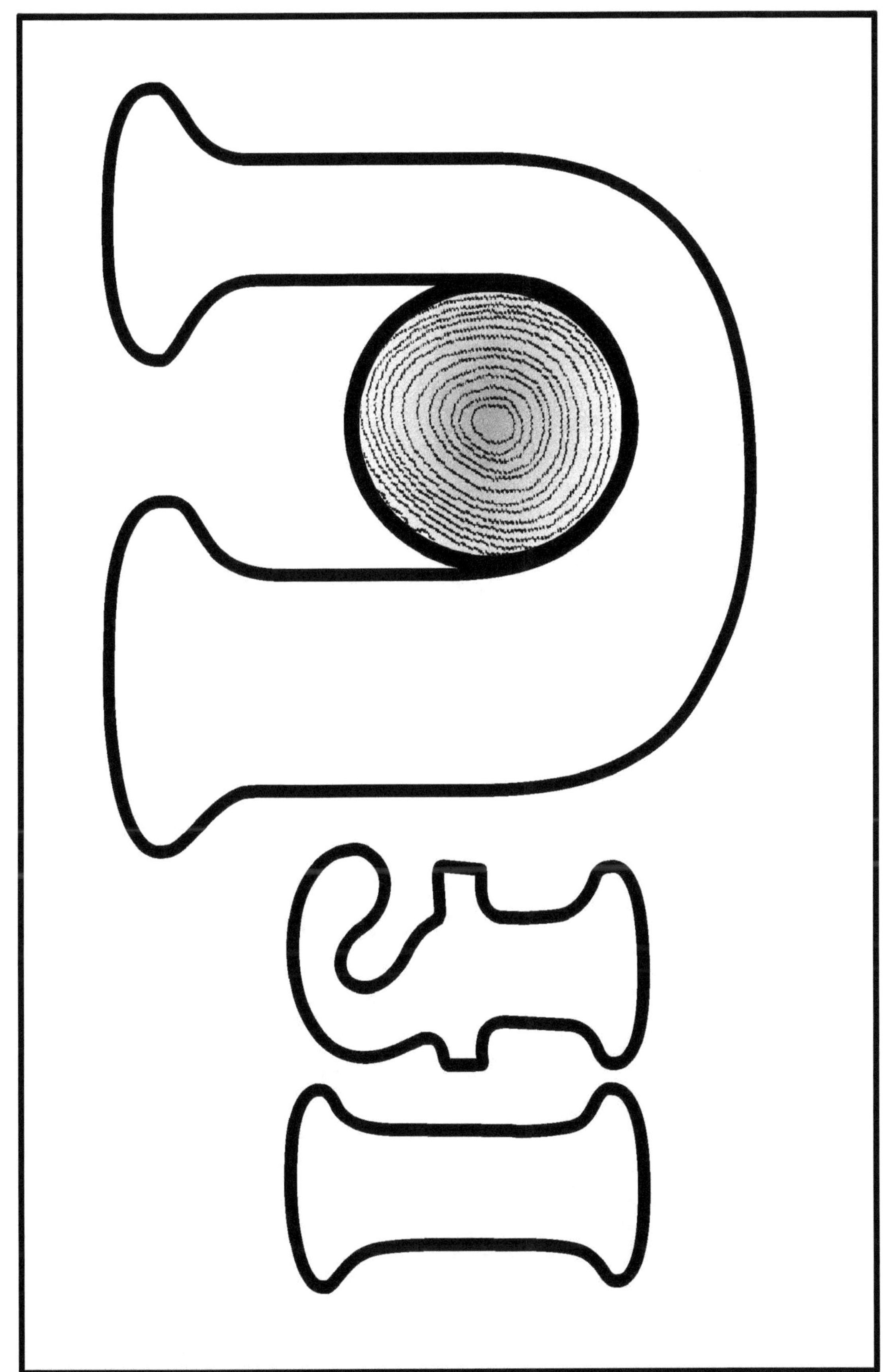

Or perhaps you may
have someone you would
like to ask the question

If Knot You ?

Then Who ?

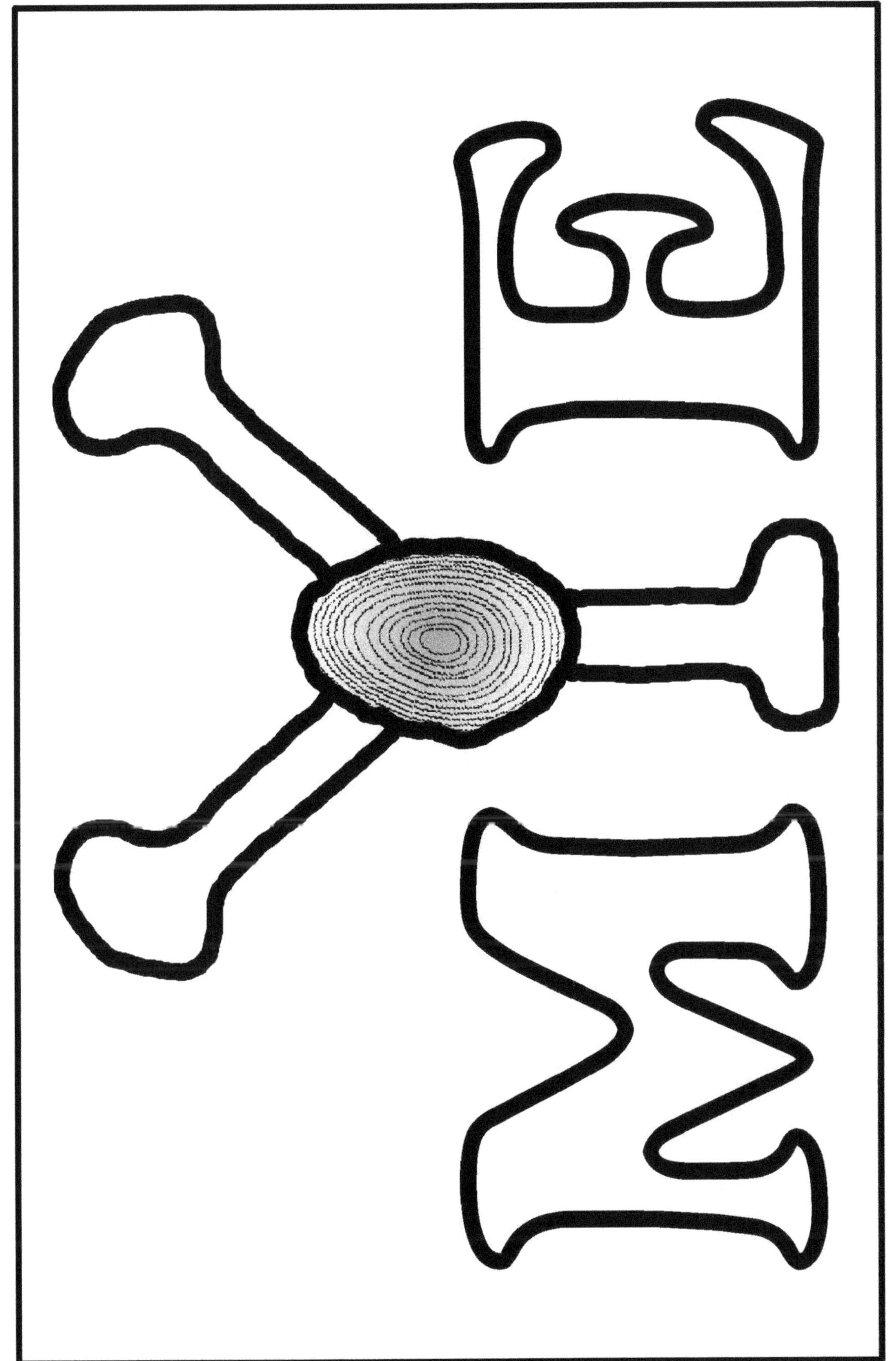

But the ultimate question you may have to ask of someone is

Y-Knot ME ?

I'm Knot into country music all that much but I do like the Judd's song

Why Not Me ?

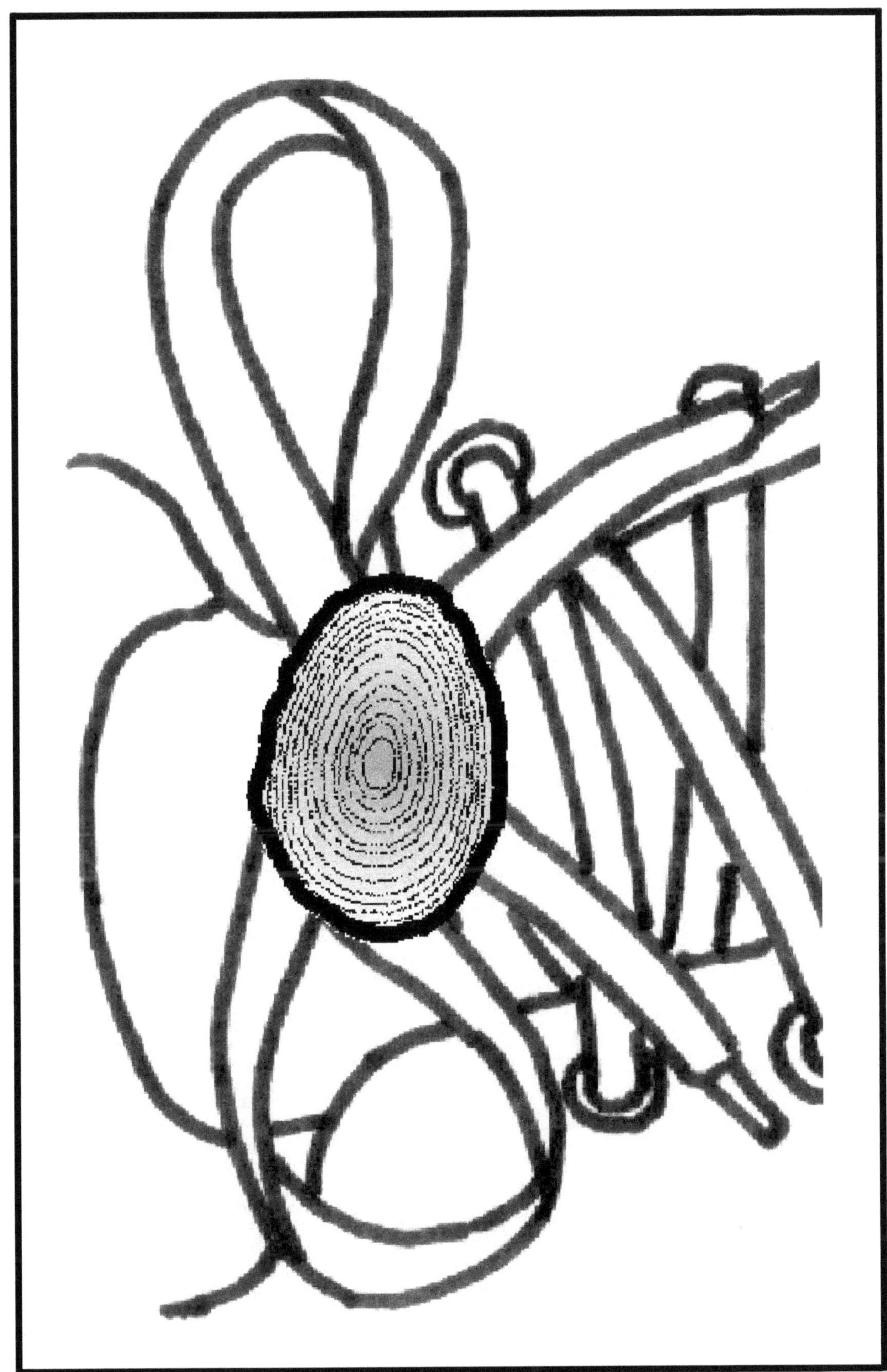

Do you believe in psychic energy ?
As I was finishing the Y-Knot ME ?
My sister Sue called and asked me
have you thought about a bow and

Tying The Knot

Yes I said, but Knot in the sense of
a "What Knot" But consider it done

As we go through life there will be people we meet that in making their acquaintance you hope that both their lives will be positively affected by the experience and hope that they

<u>Forget Me Knot</u>

In such a case you might reflect on the line from Rudyard Kipling's poem "IF"
If you can wait and Knot be tired by waiting

So if you've had a laugh or know
someone who could use a lift or
perhaps you've learned something
through all this Knotsense then

<u>**Y-Knot Buy**</u>

a copy of this book to share with a
friend or loved one or even your
significant other for them to enjoy?
Take care and Have A Great Life !

This book is dedicated to my one and only long term companion who during that time gave me the inspiration to create the "What Knots" Sharon Michelle Smollar

And to an E-Harmony acquaintance who recently has given me the inspiration and motivation to finally see the Knotsense books to their fruition Kimberly Matthews

I would also like to express my appreciation to my sister Sue who suggested several of the play on words which will be included in the future "The Book of More Knotsense" "The Book of Literary Knotsense" "The Book of Historical Knotsense" and "The Book of Modern TechKnotlogy"

A Message From the Author

If you've enjoyed the book and want to share a cartoon with a friend I just ask that you add the link to my website **www.knotsense.com** so that if they like the cartoon they can have the opportunity to purchase a full copy of the book and I'm sure you'll agree after reading it that the entertainment value is well worth the cost of having a copy for yourself to share.

Please watch for my future books:

The Book of More Knotsense
The Book of Literary Knotsense
The Book of Historical Knotsense
The Book of Modern TechKnotlogy

Order this book online at www.trafford.com/08-0432
or email orders@trafford.com

Most Trafford titles are also available at major online book retailers.

Note for Librarians: A cataloguing record for this book is available from Library and Archives Canada at www.collectionscanada.ca/amicus/index-e.html

ISBN: 978-1-4251-7520-7

We at Trafford believe that it is the responsibility of us all, as both individuals and corporations, to make choices that are environmentally and socially sound. You, in turn, are supporting this responsible conduct each time you purchase a Trafford book, or make use of our publishing services. To find out how you are helping, please visit www.trafford.com/responsiblepublishing.html

Our mission is to efficiently provide the world's finest, most comprehensive book publishing service, enabling every author to experience success. To find out how to publish your book, your way, and have it available worldwide, visit us online at www.trafford.com/10510

www.trafford.com

North America & international
toll-free: 1 888 232 4444 (USA & Canada)
phone: 250 383 6864 ♦ fax: 250 383 6804
email: info@trafford.com

The United Kingdom & Europe
phone: +44 (0)1865 722 113 ♦ local rate: 0845 230 9601
facsimile: +44 (0)1865 722 868 ♦ email: info.uk@trafford.com

10 9 8 7 6 5 4

www.ingramcontent.com/pod-product-compliance
Ingram Content Group UK Ltd.
Pitfield, Milton Keynes, MK11 3LW, UK
UKHW051129260726
13967UKWH00010B/2949